Beastly BUGS

Beastly
BUGS

Written by Steve Parker

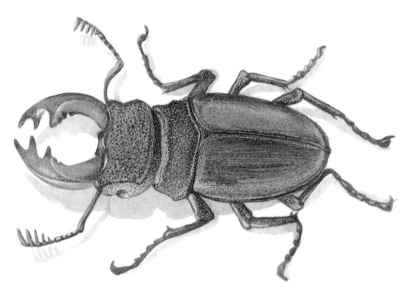

Scientific Consultant Joyce Pope
Illustrated by Ann Savage

RSVP
RAINTREE
STECK-VAUGHN
P U B L I S H E R S
The Steck-Vaughn Company

Austin, Texas

Library of Congress Cataloging-in-Publication Data
Parker, Steve.
Beastly bugs / written by Steve Parker.
p. cm. — (Creepy creatures)
Includes index.
Summary: Describes the physical characteristics and habits
of such species of insects as butterflies, fleas, beetles, and termites.
ISBN 0-8114-0689-X
ISBN 0-8114-6333-8 softcover binding
1. Insects—Juvenile literature. [1.Insects.]
1.Title. II. Series: Parker, Steve. Creepy creatures.
QL467.2.P352   1994
595.7—dc20   92-43197   CIP   AC

Editors: Wendy Madgwick, Susan Wilson
Designer: Janie Louise Hunt

Color reproduction by Global Colour, Malaysia
Printed in the United States
2 3 4 5 6 7 8 9 0 LB 98 97 96 95 94

Contents

Beastly Bugs

Our world teems with bugs, beetles, and other insects. Some are pests that sting us, bite us, or eat our crops. But most insects live quiet lives, out of our way. The insect group is the biggest in the animal kingdom, with over a million different species or kinds. You can identify an insect by the number of legs it has. When it's adult, it has six legs and most have wings. Spiders and scorpions have eight legs, and centipedes and millipedes have many more.

▼ Many insects are camouflaged and look like twigs, leaves, or flowers. This means they can hide from predators or wait secretly to pounce on their prey. The **brown leaf insect** from New Guinea looks just like a dead brown leaf.

▶ The **assassin bug** resembles a beetle, but it's a bug. It impales its prey with its sharp spearlike mouth and injects juices that digest its prey's internal organs. Then the assassin bug sucks up the soupy insides.

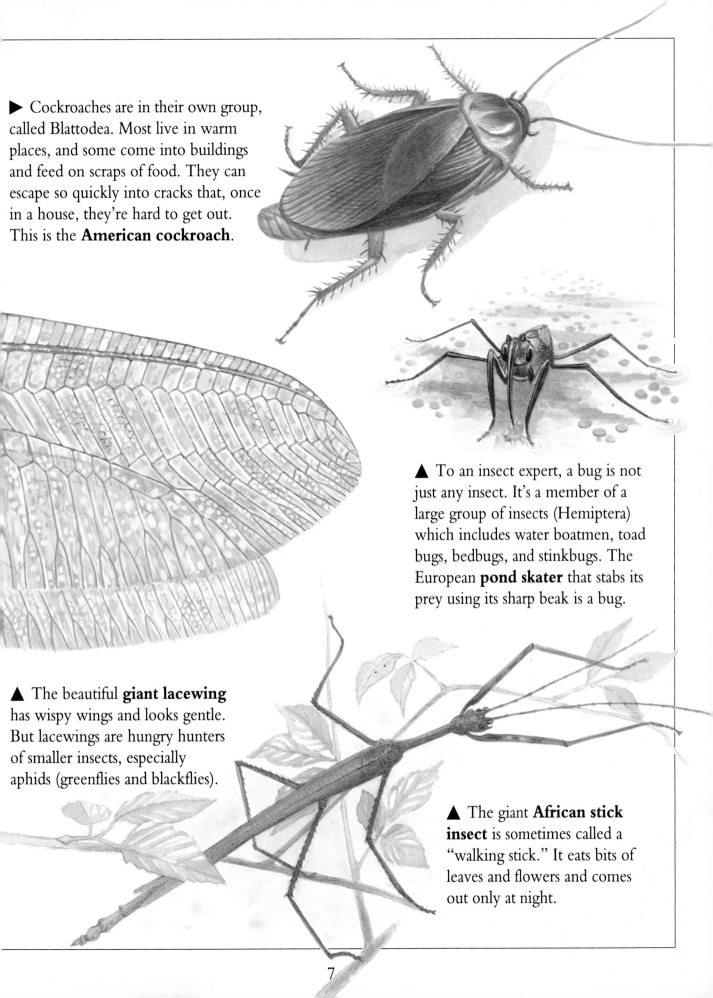

▶ Cockroaches are in their own group, called Blattodea. Most live in warm places, and some come into buildings and feed on scraps of food. They can escape so quickly into cracks that, once in a house, they're hard to get out. This is the **American cockroach**.

▲ To an insect expert, a bug is not just any insect. It's a member of a large group of insects (Hemiptera) which includes water boatmen, toad bugs, bedbugs, and stinkbugs. The European **pond skater** that stabs its prey using its sharp beak is a bug.

▲ The beautiful **giant lacewing** has wispy wings and looks gentle. But lacewings are hungry hunters of smaller insects, especially aphids (greenflies and blackflies).

▲ The giant **African stick insect** is sometimes called a "walking stick." It eats bits of leaves and flowers and comes out only at night.

Beautiful Butterflies

Butterflies are among the most colorful of all insects. The beautiful tints and patterns on their wings are made up of thousands of tiny colored scales, like a living mosaic. Most adult butterflies feed on the sweet, sugary nectar made by flowers.

▼▶ Butterflies, like this **peacock**, are good examples of how certain insects change as they grow up. The change in body shape is called metamorphosis.

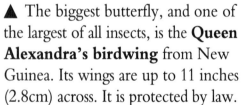

▶ **1.** The female peacock butterfly lays tiny yellowish eggs on the undersides of stinging nettle leaves.

▲ The biggest butterfly, and one of the largest of all insects, is the **Queen Alexandra's birdwing** from New Guinea. Its wings are up to 11 inches (2.8cm) across. It is protected by law.

▶ **2.** The caterpillars, or larvae, hatch from the eggs. As they eat and grow, they molt, or shed their skin, several times.

◀ **Monarch caterpillars** eat poisonous plants such as milkweed. The poison does not hurt the caterpillars, instead they store it in their bodies. Birds who eat just one will leave other monarchs alone.

4. The adult butterfly emerges from the chrysalis, spreads its wings so that they dry and harden, and then flies away.

▼ The **red admiral's** name comes from its bright colors, which were said to be "admirable." This butterfly is a good flier, but it may get drunk in the fall when it sips the juice of rotting fruit.

3. The caterpillars turn into hard-cased chrysalises, the pupa stage, that hang from a stem or tree trunk.

▶ **Monarch butterflies** fly north in spring, from Mexico and the southern United States, as far north as Canada. They breed on the way, and the new generation migrates back south, more than 1,900 miles (3,058km). Millions of monarchs rest on trees through the winter, and tourists come to marvel at them.

Marvelous Moths

There are more than 200,000 kinds of butterflies and moths in the insect group Lepidoptera. Over nine-tenths of these are moths. They are mostly small and grayish or brown. But some of them rival butterflies with their bright colors and patterns.

▶ The **cecropia** or **robin moth** lives east of the Rocky Mountains. It is one of the biggest moths in North America. Its wings are nearly 6 inches (15cm) across.

▲ Most moths fly at night, while butterflies are active during the day. But there are exceptions, like the **burnet moth**. It flits around in the sunshine, its red spots acting as a warning that it tastes horrible.

▶ Hawkmoths are big, bulky, and fast-flying. The **death's-head hawkmoth** is named after the skull-like pattern behind its head.

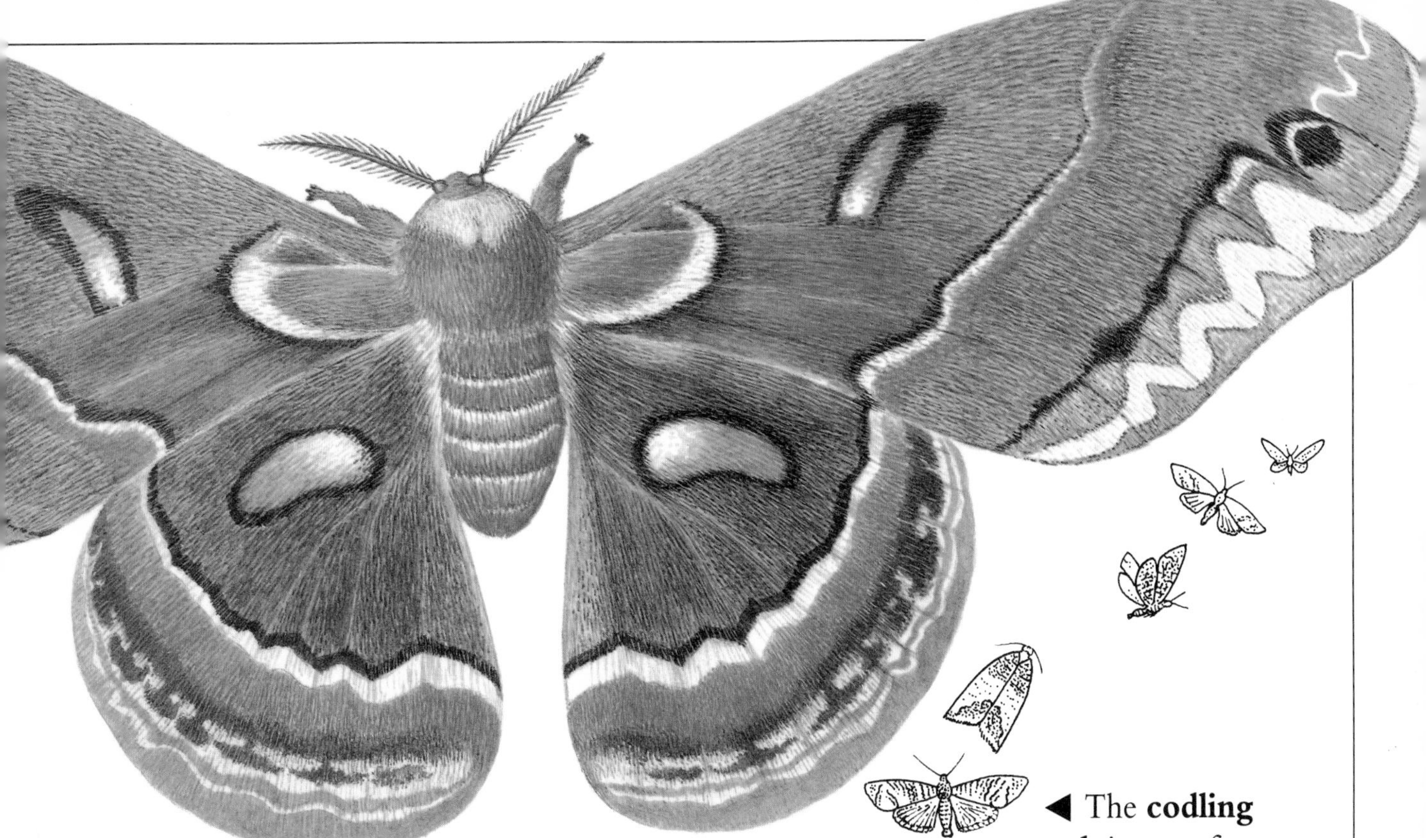

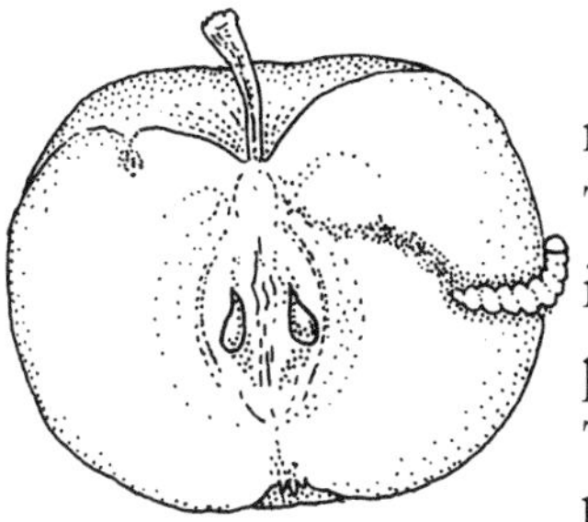

◀ The **codling moth** is one of many small, dull-colored moths that we rarely see. This one is unusual because its caterpillars eat apples, pears, and other similar fruits. The "worm" you find in a bad apple is probably a codling moth caterpillar.

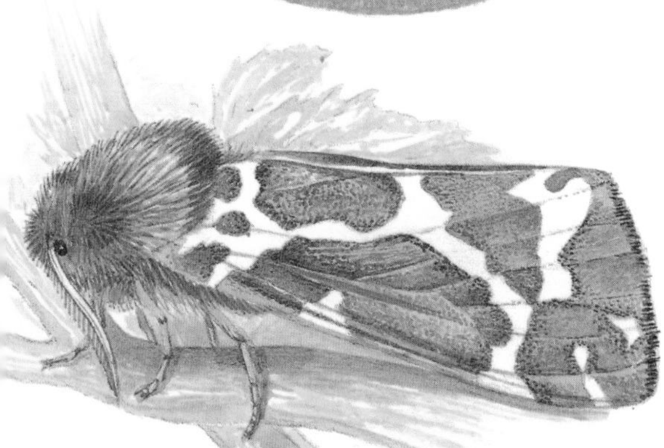

▲ Most moths hold their wings out flat when at rest, whereas butterflies fold them together over their back. But there are exceptions, like the **garden tiger moth**. It often brings its wings together over its back.

▶ The **atlas moth** from South and Southeast Asia is among the biggest moths in the world. It can measure almost a foot across the wing tips.

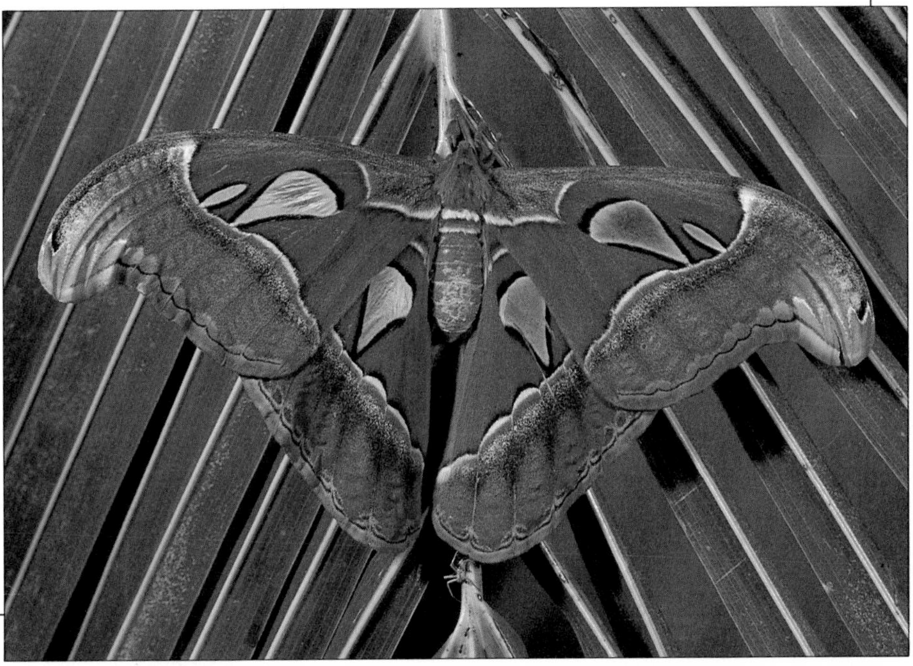

Meat-Eating Mantids

Mantids are among the fiercest hunters of all insects. A mantis is usually well camouflaged as a twig or leaf. Most of the time it sits still, waiting. But when a fly, caterpillar, or similar insect comes near — snap! The mantis flicks out its hooked front legs, grabs the prey, and begins to munch away with its strong jaws. It all happens faster than the time it takes you to blink.

▶ As a mantis watches its meal, its head turns slowly. From the angle of its head and neck, the mantis's computerlike brain works out exactly where to strike with its front legs.

▲ The **praying mantis** gets its name not because it preys on victims, but because its "hands" are folded as though in prayer.

▶ Mantids are expert ambushers. This **flower mantis** nymph from the West Indies looks like a blossom. It is waiting to pounce on any insect that comes in search of nectar.

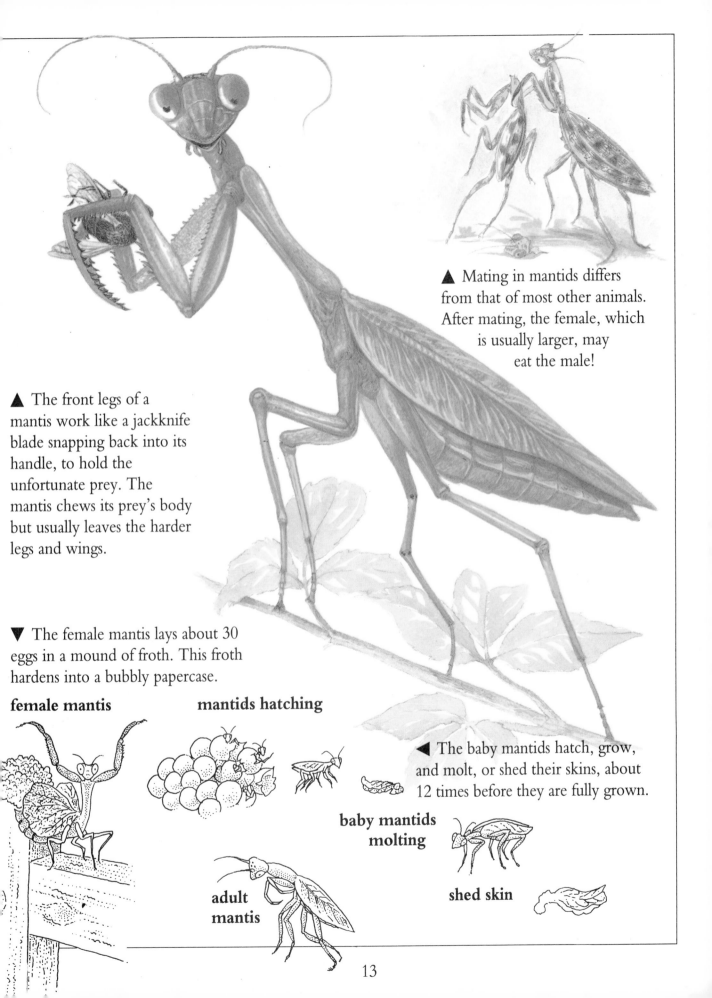

▲ Mating in mantids differs from that of most other animals. After mating, the female, which is usually larger, may eat the male!

▲ The front legs of a mantis work like a jackknife blade snapping back into its handle, to hold the unfortunate prey. The mantis chews its prey's body but usually leaves the harder legs and wings.

▼ The female mantis lays about 30 eggs in a mound of froth. This froth hardens into a bubbly papercase.

female mantis

mantids hatching

◀ The baby mantids hatch, grow, and molt, or shed their skins, about 12 times before they are fully grown.

baby mantids molting

adult mantis

shed skin

Irritating Insects

On a hot day, irritating insects seem to be everywhere. Flies buzz around, often spreading germs. Mosquitoes try to suck your blood. If you are not careful, even more problems arise — ants get in your pants, fleas on your skin, and lice in your hair! Here are some of the peskier members of the insect world that we could sometimes do without.

adult louse

hair

nit

▶ Tiny and flattened, **fleas** are brown specks, not much larger than this period. But they bite and suck blood and cause red marks, swelling, and itching in your skin. Different types of fleas live on cats, dogs, chickens, and people.

▲ **Lice** are small, pale insects that specialize in bloodsucking. Their eggs, called "nits," resemble grains of salt and are usually attached to hairs.

mosquito piercing skin

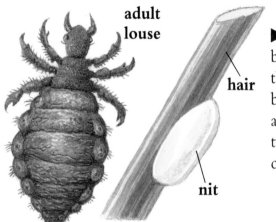

◀▲ Some kinds of flies, called **mosquitoes**, pierce your skin and suck your blood with their hollow, needlelike mouths. There are thousands of kinds of these tiny flies. A few spread horrible diseases — malaria, yellow fever, dog heartworm, and elephantiasis.

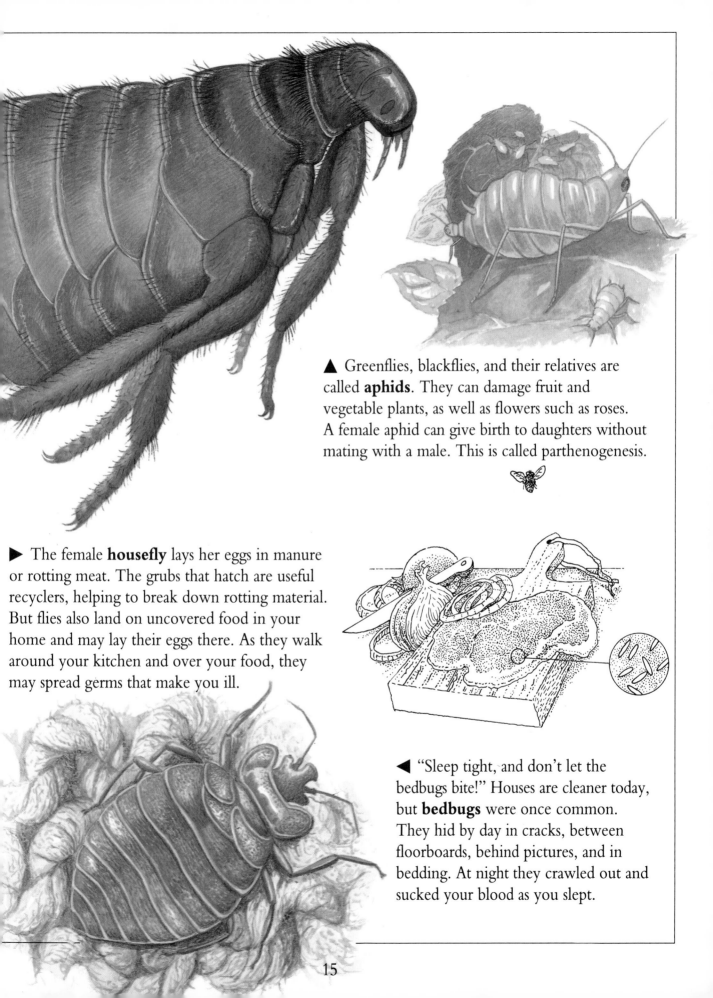

▲ Greenflies, blackflies, and their relatives are called **aphids**. They can damage fruit and vegetable plants, as well as flowers such as roses. A female aphid can give birth to daughters without mating with a male. This is called parthenogenesis.

▶ The female **housefly** lays her eggs in manure or rotting meat. The grubs that hatch are useful recyclers, helping to break down rotting material. But flies also land on uncovered food in your home and may lay their eggs there. As they walk around your kitchen and over your food, they may spread germs that make you ill.

◀ "Sleep tight, and don't let the bedbugs bite!" Houses are cleaner today, but **bedbugs** were once common. They hid by day in cracks, between floorboards, behind pictures, and in bedding. At night they crawled out and sucked your blood as you slept.

15

Fearsome Flies

Many insects have four wings. True flies have only one pair of wings. Each of the rear wings has become a haltere, a tiny stick with a ball on the end. Halteres seem to help the fly keep its balance. There are over 100,000 kinds of flies, and a few are harmful.

◀▶ After several years in the soil, the maggotlike leatherjacket turns into a pupa. This changes into a long-legged **cranefly**. Its halteres look like mini-gyroscopes.

leatherjacket

cranefly

haltere

▶ Beware of the female **horsefly**. She can bite through a horse's thick skin to suck its blood, so your thin skin is easy to pierce. But don't worry if it's a male horsefly, it eats only nectar and pollen from flowers. The trouble is, they are very difficult to tell apart!

◀ **Robber-flies** are big, fierce-looking flies that lie in wait on a twig or leaf. They dart out to catch smaller insects such as mosquitoes, gnats, and midges.

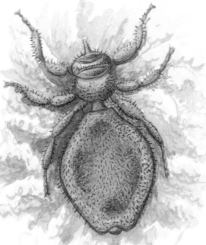

▲ **Sheep bot-flies** lay their eggs on or near the head of a sheep. The maggots live in the sheep's nose and air passages, often causing great pain.

▶ **Dung flies** buzz around cowpats, horse droppings, and other kinds of manure. They lay their eggs in fresh, warm dung. The maggots, or larvae, hatch out and eat the dung. The well-fed maggots turn into pupae from which adult flies emerge. Without dung flies, dung beetles, and many other living things that break down dung, we would be knee-deep in droppings.

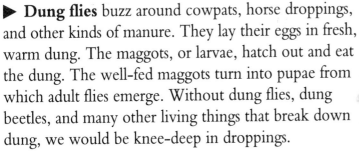

◀ The **cow warble-fly** lays its eggs under a cow's skin. The maggots hatch out of the eggs, and burrow into the cow and feed on its flesh. Later they drop to the ground, turn into pupae, and then become adult flies.

Greedy Grasshoppers...

Buzz-buzz-buzz, chirp-chirp-chirp, greep-greep-greep. The summer air is full of the sounds of crickets grasshoppers, katydids, and their kin. The sounds are usually made by the males calling to females, to mate with them. Though we hear these insects, we rarely see them unless we walk through the tall grass.

◀ The **field cricket** sings by scraping a comblike part of its front wing over a thick vein, or tube, on the other front wing. Sometimes a male cricket attacks another male that comes too close. Some Asian countries hold cricket-fighting competitions.

◀ **Grasshoppers** and crickets make enormous leaps using their long, powerful back legs. When they jump away from a predator, they often open their bright wings in a flash of color — then close them again and land unseen.

and Chirping Crickets

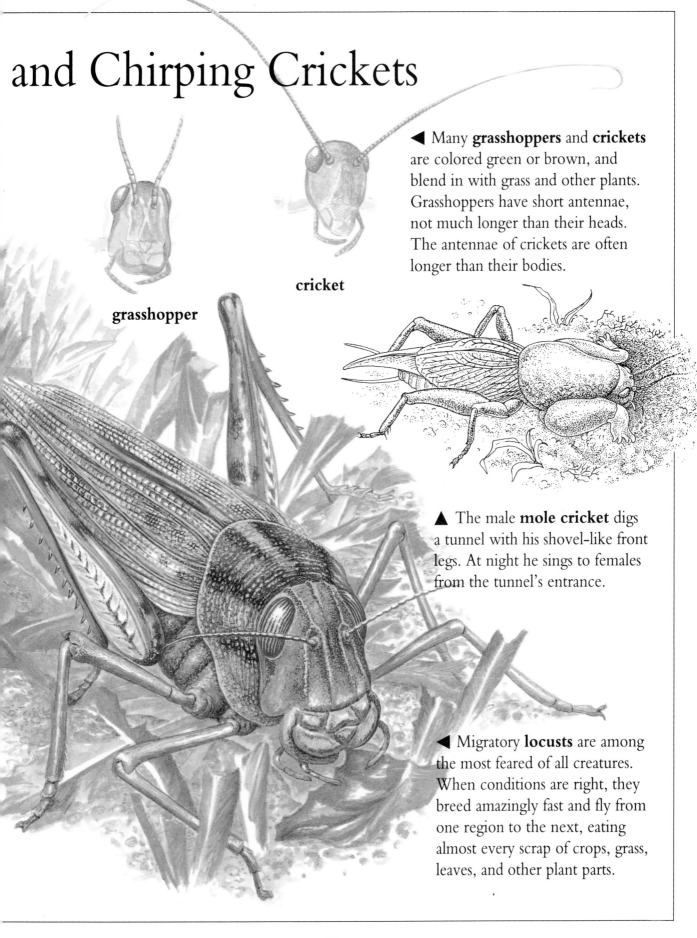

grasshopper

cricket

◀ Many **grasshoppers** and **crickets** are colored green or brown, and blend in with grass and other plants. Grasshoppers have short antennae, not much longer than their heads. The antennae of crickets are often longer than their bodies.

▲ The male **mole cricket** digs a tunnel with his shovel-like front legs. At night he sings to females from the tunnel's entrance.

◀ Migratory **locusts** are among the most feared of all creatures. When conditions are right, they breed amazingly fast and fly from one region to the next, eating almost every scrap of crops, grass, leaves, and other plant parts.

Darting Dragonflies

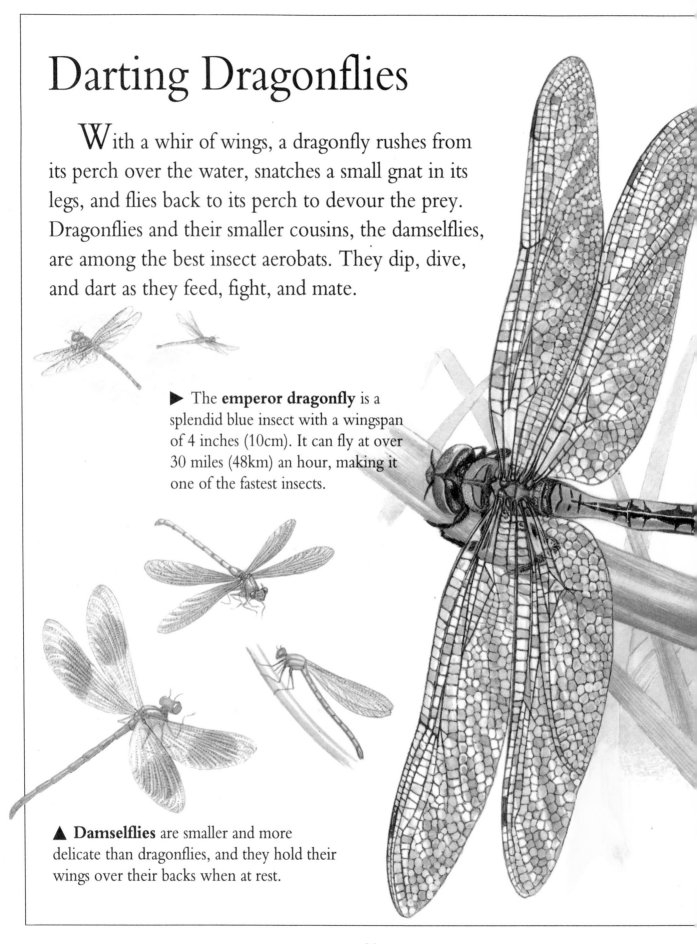

With a whir of wings, a dragonfly rushes from its perch over the water, snatches a small gnat in its legs, and flies back to its perch to devour the prey. Dragonflies and their smaller cousins, the damselflies, are among the best insect aerobats. They dip, dive, and dart as they feed, fight, and mate.

▶ The **emperor dragonfly** is a splendid blue insect with a wingspan of 4 inches (10cm). It can fly at over 30 miles (48km) an hour, making it one of the fastest insects.

▲ **Damselflies** are smaller and more delicate than dragonflies, and they hold their wings over their backs when at rest.

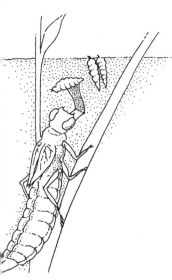

◀ Dragonflies and damselflies begin life as eggs, laid in or near water. These eggs hatch into a form called the **naiad**, which lives in ponds, streams, and lakes. The naiads are powerful predators that eat tadpoles, worms, pond snails, and tiny fish.

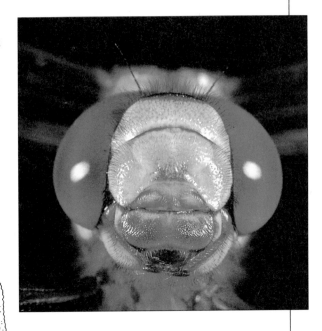

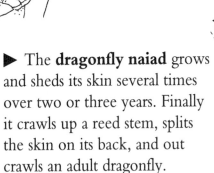

▶ The **dragonfly naiad** grows and sheds its skin several times over two or three years. Finally it crawls up a reed stem, splits the skin on its back, and out crawls an adult dragonfly.

▲ Most insects have multipart eyes that give them good eyesight. **Dragonflies** hunt by sight, and their eyes are bigger and better than most other insects. Each eye has up to 30,000 separate lenses, that probably see a mosaic view of the world.

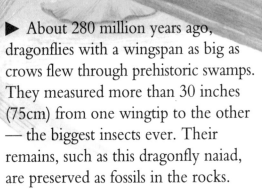

▶ About 280 million years ago, dragonflies with a wingspan as big as crows flew through prehistoric swamps. They measured more than 30 inches (75cm) from one wingtip to the other — the biggest insects ever. Their remains, such as this dragonfly naiad, are preserved as fossils in the rocks.

Termite Towers

Termites are the most important recyclers of dead vegetation in warm parts of the world. Their activity helps to keep the soil fertile. Unfortunately for us, the dry wood of buildings and furniture are food for some kinds of termites. They can cause millions of dollars' worth of damage.

▶ **Termites** are sometimes called "white ants." And like ants, they live in colonies in huge nests, such as the tower shown here. But termites are *not* a kind of ant. They have their own insect group called Isoptera.

Air passing up the central chimney cools the tower.

Air-conditioning side tunnels.

Walls are made of baked, hard mud.

Royal chamber with queen and workers.

Food stores of rotten wood and fungus.

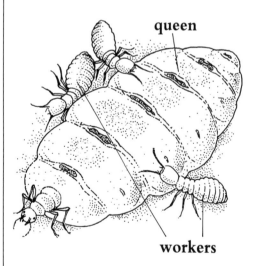

queen

workers

▲ A **queen termite's** workers that serve as courtiers attend to her every need, for she is little more than a swollen bag of eggs. She may lay as many as 4 million eggs a year.

▲ **Termites** are soft, pale, moist, and blind. They need to stay underground or in damp places to survive. The soldier termites (see above) have jaws like huge pincers, ready to attack enemies, mainly ants.

Termite eggs and grubs (nymphs) in nursery chambers.

Main nest areas are below ground level.

▲ The **magnetic termites** of Australia always build their tall, thin nests facing north–south. It was thought they had tiny compasses to help them! But they may sense direction from the apparent movement of the sun across the sky.

Boring Beetles

Insects make up the biggest group of animals, and beetles make up the biggest group of insects. There are more than 300,000 kinds around the world, living in almost every habitat, from mountain tops to deserts, lakes, and forests. Many lay eggs that hatch into wood-eating grubs, which bore into trees and wooden structures.

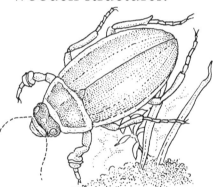

◀ This strong, tough beetle lives most of its life under water, breathing air trapped under its wing cases, and preying on small fish, tadpoles, and worms. It's the **great diving beetle**.

▼ A beetle's front wings are hard, domed cases that cover the top of its body. These wing cases protect the larger, delicate flying wings folded beneath. In flight the wing cases are held out of the way, as in this **cockchafer**.

▲ The heaviest insect is the **goliath beetle** from central Africa. It grows to over 4 inches (10cm) long and weighs over 3 1/2 ounces (100g).

24

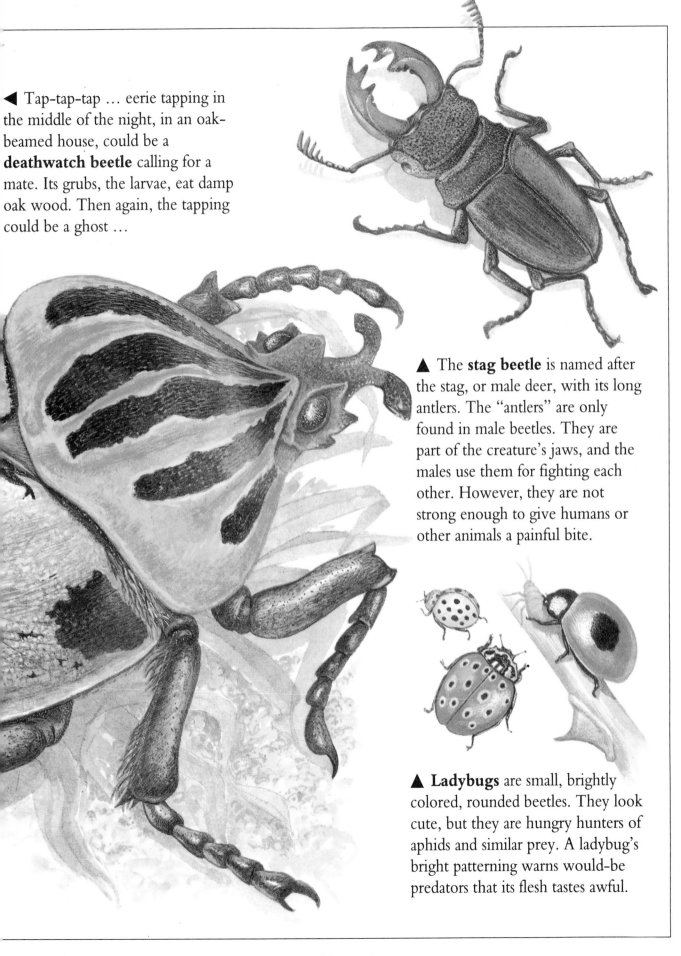

◄ Tap-tap-tap … eerie tapping in the middle of the night, in an oak-beamed house, could be a **deathwatch beetle** calling for a mate. Its grubs, the larvae, eat damp oak wood. Then again, the tapping could be a ghost …

▲ The **stag beetle** is named after the stag, or male deer, with its long antlers. The "antlers" are only found in male beetles. They are part of the creature's jaws, and the males use them for fighting each other. However, they are not strong enough to give humans or other animals a painful bite.

▲ **Ladybugs** are small, brightly colored, rounded beetles. They look cute, but they are hungry hunters of aphids and similar prey. A ladybug's bright patterning warns would-be predators that its flesh tastes awful.

Busy Bees...

Watch out, there's a wasp! We soon learn to recognize the bright yellow and black stripes of some bees, wasps, and hornets. So do other animals. We know that the stripes mean danger, in the form of a sharp stinger. Honeybees live in a hive or nest, and so do common wasps. But most other bees and wasps live on their own.

bee "dancing" on hive

▲ When a **honeybee** finds a good patch of flowers, or another source of food, it flies back to the hive and "dances" on the comb. The dance's direction and the number of body waggles tell the other bees where the flowers are.

▶ **Bumblebees** live in smaller groups than honeybees. They make their nests under the ground, digging tunnels and chambers in soft soil. They often use the old nests of mice to save themselves from doing too much digging.

and Worrying Wasps

► This **wasps'** nest is about the size of a soccer ball and is the home for 5,000 members of the colony. It is made of thin, flaky "paper" that the wasps produce by chewing wood and mixing it with their saliva (spit).

larvae (grubs) in cells

outer wall of nest

pupae in cells

eggs in cells

queen lays eggs

cross-section of wasp's nest

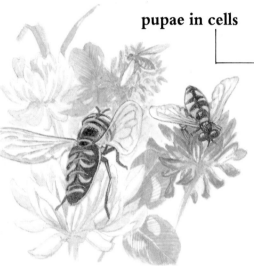

▲ The harmless **hoverfly** mimics, or looks like, a bee or wasp with its yellow or black stripes. Mimicry, or looking like something else, protects the hoverfly from being attacked or eaten by other animals.

▼ The **hornet** is a very large type of wasp. It flies slowly with a droning noise. This usually peaceful insect can deliver a painful sting.

Acid Ants

Ants are close relatives of bees and wasps. They all belong to the insect group called Hymenoptera. They are tiny but busy, living in large, well-organized colonies. Worker ants fetch food and clean and repair the nest. Soldier ants bite invaders with their big jaws or squirt them with stinging acid. Only the queen ant usually lays eggs, and special worker ants feed and clean her.

▼ **Wood ants** make anthills of twigs, leaves, and soil. There might be 300,000 workers and several queen ants in a big anthill.

▶ Big ants can give you a painful nip with their strong, pincerlike jaws. Some ants, like the **wood ant**, squirt formic acid from their rear end, which stings the enemy.

▶ When the weather is right, hordes of **black garden ants** fly from their nests, under the pavement and in the ground. They are winged males and females. They mate, the males die, and the females go off to start new nests.

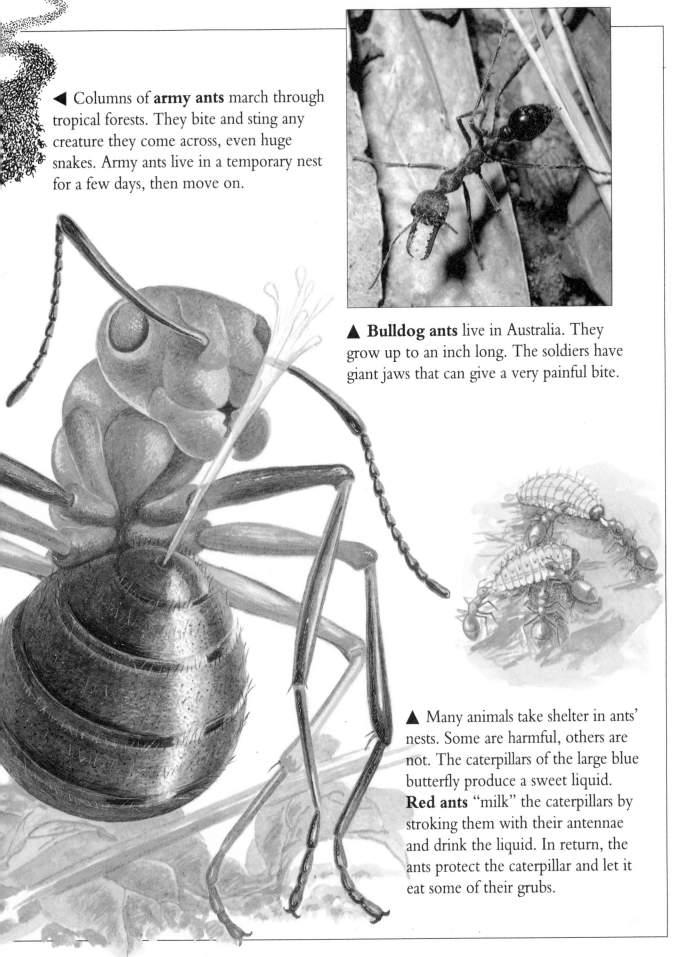

◀ Columns of **army ants** march through tropical forests. They bite and sting any creature they come across, even huge snakes. Army ants live in a temporary nest for a few days, then move on.

▲ **Bulldog ants** live in Australia. They grow up to an inch long. The soldiers have giant jaws that can give a very painful bite.

▲ Many animals take shelter in ants' nests. Some are harmful, others are not. The caterpillars of the large blue butterfly produce a sweet liquid. **Red ants** "milk" the caterpillars by stroking them with their antennae and drink the liquid. In return, the ants protect the caterpillar and let it eat some of their grubs.

Scurrying Centipedes

Lift up a log or stone in a summer woodland, and you'll probably see a centipede or two dash for cover. These creatures are not bugs, or even insects. They are in their own animal group, Chilopoda, which is related to millipedes, spiders, and insects. All centipedes are fast, active hunters, with a poisonous bite.

▶ The **giant centipedes** from India and Southeast Asia are the biggest in the centipede group. They grow to more than a foot long.

▶ A **centipede** does not bite with its real jaws. It attacks with its specially modified front legs, shaped like long fangs. Small centipedes rarely hurt people. But a bite from a large centipede can be more painful than a bee's sting.

▲ A centipede has two legs (one pair) on each body segment, or section. This is the **common centipede** from woods, gardens, and backyards.

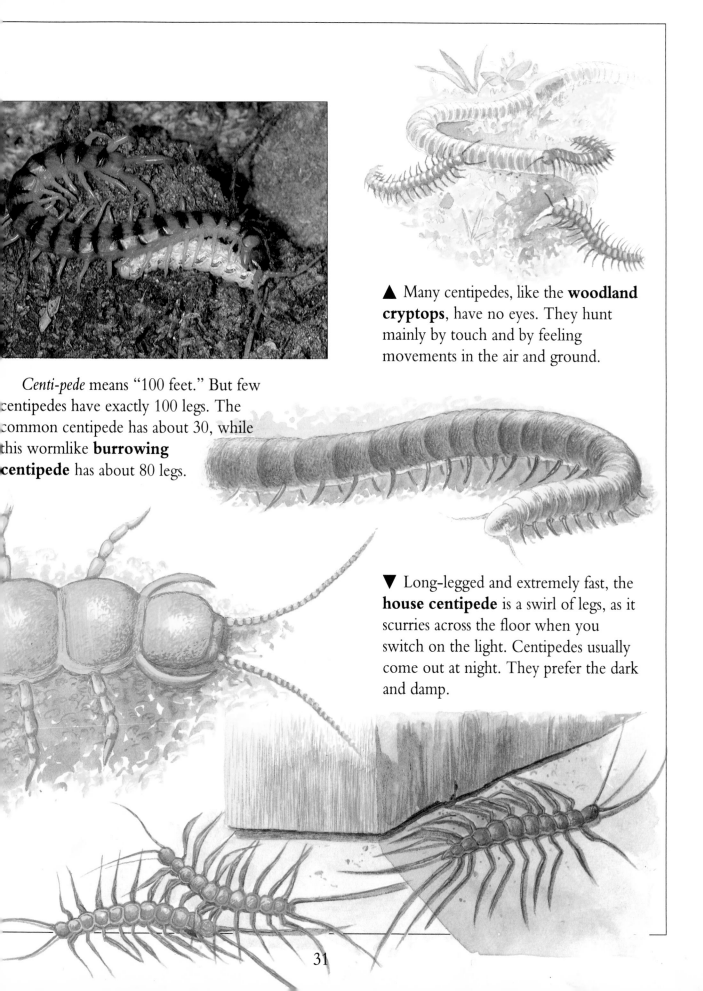

▲ Many centipedes, like the **woodland cryptops**, have no eyes. They hunt mainly by touch and by feeling movements in the air and ground.

Centi-pede means "100 feet." But few centipedes have exactly 100 legs. The common centipede has about 30, while this wormlike **burrowing centipede** has about 80 legs.

▼ Long-legged and extremely fast, the **house centipede** is a swirl of legs, as it scurries across the floor when you switch on the light. Centipedes usually come out at night. They prefer the dark and damp.

Milling Millipedes

When you lift up that log or stone in a summer forest to look for centipedes, you may also see several millipedes milling about. They do not like light and dryness, so they amble toward the nearest dark, damp crevice. Millipedes are close cousins of centipedes, but they differ in several ways …

▶ Centipedes run off or fight back when attacked. A millipede like this **pillbug** is more likely to roll into a ball. Its hard, outer body casing protects its soft legs and underside.

uncurled

rolled up

▶ The biggest **millipedes** come from tropical regions in Africa and Southeast Asia. They grow to almost a foot in length.

▲ Centipedes are carnivores (meat-eaters). **Millipedes** are herbivores — they munch on soft stems, roots, old leaves, bits of wood and bark, and other plant material.

▶ Unlike their centipede relatives, millipedes do not have a poisonous bite. But they can make a foul smell or a horrible-tasting fluid, to repel predators. In the **spotted snake millipede**, this liquid oozes from the bright spots along its sides.

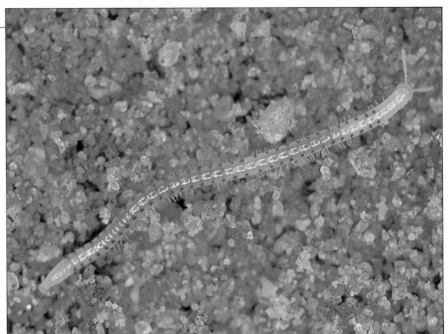

▼ Centipedes have one pair of legs on each body segment. Millipedes have two pairs of legs for each body segment. Some have beautiful body casings, like the **flatbacked millipede**.

▶ One similarity between millipedes and centipedes is that both are *not* insects. Millipedes have their own group, Diplopoda. The red legs of this **giant African millipede** warn that it tastes awful.

Glossary

Antennae The two "feelers" on an insect's head, usually near the eyes. They detect smells and air movements.

Bug In everyday language, a general name for any insect (see **Insect**). More accurately, a bug is a member of the huge bug family of insects, scientific name Hemiptera. This includes water boatmen, water striders, frog-hoppers, bedbugs, and aphids (greenfly, blackfly).

Camouflage Colored and patterned to merge and blend in with the surroundings.

Carnivore An animal that eats mainly meat or parts of animal bodies.

Caterpillar A common name for the larva of a butterfly or moth. (See **Life cycle**.)

Chrysalis A common name for the pupa of a butterfly or moth. (See **Life cycle**.)

Eggs Small rounded objects, laid by a female animal, from which the young animals grow. Insect eggs are usually pinhead-sized colored spots laid on leaves, in cracks and crevices, or under the ground. (See **Life cycle**.)

Grub A common name for an insect larva, especially of a fly. (See **Life cycle**.)

Halteres Tiny ball-and-stick balancers just behind the wings of a fly. They seem to help the insect to balance and fly steadily.

Herbivore An animal that eats mainly plants.

Insect A small animal which has six jointed legs and a hard body casing in its adult form. Most insects have two or four wings. (See also **Life cycle**.)

Larva The stage that follows the egg in the life cycle of an insect. The larva is usually active and eats a lot. (See **Life cycle**.)

Life cycle The stages that a living thing goes through during its life. In an insect it begins with the egg. In some insects this hatches into a larva, also called a maggot, grub, nymph, or caterpillar. The larva changes into a pupa, or chrysalis. From this emerges the adult or fully grown insect. (See also **Egg**, **Larva**, and **Pupa**.)

Maggot A common name for an insect larva, especially of a fly. (See **Life cycle**.)

Metamorphosis The change in body shape that is a natural part of an animal's life. Tadpoles change into frogs. Caterpillars change into chrysalises, which then change into adult moths or butterflies.

Mimicry Looking like something else. In nature, a harmless animal may look like a harmful one and avoid being eaten by other animals.

Molt When an animal casts off its body covering and grows a replacement. Insects split their body casing, crawl out and enlarge, and then a new, bigger casing forms and hardens.

Nymph The young form of some types of insects, such as grasshoppers and dragonflies. (See **Life cycle**.)

Parthenogenesis When a female animal lays eggs or gives birth to young, without having first mated with a male.

Predator An animal that hunts other animals for food.

Prey An animal that is hunted for food by other animals.

Pupa The stage in the life cycle of an insect that follows the larva stage. (See **Life cycle**.)

Segment A body section of an animal.

Warning colors Bright colors and patterns that make an animal easy to see. They warn that the animal is dangerous or tastes bad.

Index

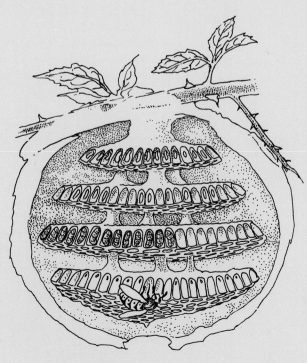

A TEMPLAR BOOK

Devised and produced by The Templar Company plc
Pippbrook Mill, London Road, Dorking,
Surrey RH4 1JE, Great Britain
Copyright © 1993 by The Templar Company plc

PHOTOGRAPHIC CREDITS
t = top, b = bottom, l = left, r = right
All photographs are from Frank Lane Picture Agency (FLPA)
page 8 Preston-Mafham/Premaphotos/FLPA; *page 9* R. Austing/FLPA;
page 11 T. de Zylva/FLPA; *page 12* Premaphotos/FLPA; *page 17*
Silvestris/FLPA; *page 18* A.R Hamblin/FLPA; *page 21t* M. Wender/
Silvestris/FLPA; *page 21b* Heather Angel/FLPA; *page 23* Preston-
Mafham/Premaphotos/FLPA; *page 24* Preston-Mafham/Premaphotos/
FLPA; *page 27* R. Cramm/Silvestris/FLPA; *page 29* Preston-Mafham/
Premaphotos/FLPA; *page 31* B. Borrell/FLPA; *page 32t* D. Jones/FLPA;
page 32b Preston-Mafham/Premaphotos/FLPA